Third Eye Awakening

A Beginner's Guide to

Awakening the Third Eye

Table of Contents

Introduction

Today, if you have found your way to reading this book, you may be going through a phase where nothing feels exactly 'right'. It may be an unfruitful job, or a failing relationship, or it may have nothing to do with external events at all. Different things happen in our lives, but when we cannot connect to our innermost selves, we feel that we are strangers to our own experiences. This can cause a lot of discontent and unhappiness. So what do you say to going on a journey with me? Spirituality goes far beyond the idea of a sage sitting cross-legged and meditating in the mountains. If that is something that you're up for, by all means, go for it. But, that is not one and all. Establishing a connection with yourself doesn't require you to go through extreme suffering or dire living situations. It simply requires faith and discipline.

A summons to greater consciousness and mental awareness is referred to as a spiritual awakening. Personal transformation and a shift in one's worldview and conceptual framework occur as a result of spiritual awakening.

Spiritual awakening is associated with an increase in one's awareness and capability to produce and receive love energy. We connect and ultimately unite with higher portions of ourselves primarily through our open mind and enlarged consciousness. It's like your consciousness blossoming into a fuller, more beautiful form. It's as if you're discovering a new planet, or hearing music for the first time.

Man is frequently portrayed as a pre-programmed automatic machine with the operator dozing off. When the operator wakes up and takes control of the steering wheel, this is called awakening. We expand our consciousness beyond our apparent physical realm of activity during spiritual awakening. As we open and live more through our hearts, we progress into the heart awareness. In this way, we gradually bring higher aspects of ourselves into consciousness, such as our intuition, soul, and Higher Self (spirit). While the soul reflects through our personality, the spirit enables us to establish contact with spiritual realms, with things that are greater and beyond mere physical existence. We are becoming increasingly aware of these aspects of the self and communicating with them.

Simultaneously, we notice a progressive shift on all other levels, including physical, emotional, cerebral, and energy/light. When we look at things from an energy standpoint, we raise our energy vibration as we progress spiritually. Everything vibrates to some extent. Matter, for example, vibrates at a very low level in comparison to sound and light, whereas loving thoughts and feelings vibrate at a very high level in comparison to selfish thoughts and feelings. As we raise our energy vibration, we begin to radiate light and raise the energy frequency of everything around us, including people and physical matter. Your heart, mind, and body become heavenly carriers.

Awakening is, at its core, the death of one's illusory sense of self. It is an intentional movement away from a false identity that takes us back to the essence of who we are. This fake identity is whatever you're referring to when you speak the word "I" before Awakening. When people say "I," they usually refer to themselves as a distinct individual with a distinct set of experiences. This person defines who they believe they are, which I refer to as the ego.

We believe that we are this self before Awakening, which perceives itself as inherently distinct from everyone and everything else. The truth is that we are all undifferentiated and undivided representations of One Consciousness. An infinite multiplicity of simultaneous experiences arises inside this One Consciousness, and a common element of these experiences is a sense of identity, a sense of "I." Someone who is "Awake" has lost their core sense of "I" (although there will usually be residues of ego or "shadow-I's" floating around, which will be dealt with over time).

When people first hear this, they typically assume that somebody who has lost his sense of "I" must have died, gone insane, or turned into a bland, shallow husk of a person. This isn't the case at all. Consider the following scenario: ever since you were a baby, you've always believed you were a reindeer.. As a result, you've lived your entire life acting like a reindeer to the best of your ability.

When you were hungry, you ate grass off the lawn; instead of talking, you would snort and shake your imaginary mane; and if someone enraged you, you would make an effort to charge them with the horns ostensibly sprouting from the sides of your head. You would be an adult who had only ever known himself as a reindeer by the time you were in your thirties. If it occurred to you that you might not be a reindeer after all, the idea would be terrifying—imagining what it would be like to not be a reindeer after so many years would be practically impossible. Despite your fears, it is evident that it is in your best interests to let go of your reindeer identity and live as who you truly are. If you were to eventually view yourself as a human, you might not know how to act at first because you have never acted like one before, and all of your reindeer traits would be deeply embedded in your behavior. It might take some time for you to fully realize your humanity, and you would probably continue to act like a reindeer in the meantime, but the illusion has been broken. You're well aware that you're a human, and it will only be a matter of time before you start acting like one. It may be a difficult process, but no matter how happy you thought you were as a reindeer, you certainly need to go through this transformation for your own mental and emotional well-being. Obviously, this is an extreme and outlandish example, but it demonstrates the point well.

So, as we move on, you will realize that awakening your inner being is the key to understanding who you truly are and what your purpose in life is. You may have been deluded into living your life in terms of certain specifics. It's time to change that and understand and accept your true self.

Chapter 1: What Is the Third Eye?

The *ajna chakra*, to understand from a spiritual standpoint, is the third eye. Our bodies have seven energy centers where nerve points meet. The *ajna chakra* is a place of energy placed between our brows. This point is linked to intuition, or the ability to detect things beyond the five senses.

The pituitary and hypothalamus glands are associated with the *ajna chakra*. When our brain is perceiving different things, it emits distinct waves.

When we feel peaceful, relaxed, or deeply happy, we produce alpha waves. The vibrations of alpha waves are calmer, and they act as a sonar. Dolphins' brains are known to have a high level of alpha wave function, which aids in their navigation in the sea. Their sonar functions in a similar way to that of a submarine. Physically, the pituitary and hypothalamic glands' softness allows alpha waves to spread.

The most powerful waves are gamma waves, which can be felt in a deep meditative state known as *samadhi*.

When our bodies are in tune with nature, our brain produces alpha waves. When one's behaviors and thoughts are in sync with nature, one's entire self feels as if it is a part of the cosmos. As a result, when a person's alpha wave activity is high, nature discloses certain things to them. This is commonly referred to as intuition. The experience of gamma wave emission occurs only when we have frequent alpha wave emissions in our subtle body, the inner expression of our beings. The *ajna chakra* is activated by gamma wave emissions. We feel a sense of lightness in our heads when the third eye activates.

The *ajna chakra* is the sixth of the seven chakras' energy centers. The freedom of thought and speech occurs when this chakra is in balance. Every chakra is linked to a particular color, much as we link our birth months to certain stones. Indigo is the hue that best represents this chakra. Royal blue or dark blue tones are linked with inner divinity. Therefore, indigo also allows access to the Divine. The color indigo is associated with wisdom and inner knowledge. It brings clarity to all of the body's five senses. Indigo is a color that promotes the transition of lower chakra energy into higher spiritual vibrations.

This Chakra is firmly linked to supreme wisdom and spiritual enlightenment. It is a conduit to higher awareness and channels energy towards universal wisdom.

The third eye chakra is positioned in the center of your head, between your brows. The third eye provides insight into the future, whereas the two physical eyes observe the present. Our physical eyes are also the maps to our past, because the past and present are inherently linked; the former cannot exist without the formation of the latter. Through inner vision, this chakra establishes a connection with the outside world. Focusing on the third eye inspires us to rise above worldly lust and diversions. *Ajna* means 'perception,' but it can also imply 'become aware of,' and 'control.'

When this Chakra is out of balance, you are more prone to rigidity, wrath, judgement, and non-acceptance of individuals and situations that are different. A blocked Third Eye Chakra also makes you fearful of actual achievement and attaining your goals since you'll have to give up your identity and become someone else in the process.

When your *ajna chakra* is in harmony, you can accurately observe and understand yourself. You will have the ability to make the best decisions and make accurate judgments of people and situations. You may see the "truth" that surrounds us simply by using the power of your mind and intuition.

However, too much of something good can become bad! You might live in a fantasy world if your *ajna chakra* is overactive. You can become disconnected from reality and find it difficult to live your life. You may believe that life is unfair and that the world is to blame for your issues. This can cause disorientation, depression, and focus issues. You can even have hallucinations and misinterpret everyday situations. You may become judgmental and overly analytical in your thoughts.

When your *ajna chakra* is inactive, you will find it difficult to think for yourself, and you will rely on authorities to make decisions for you. You will create a rigid mindset and place an excessive amount of faith in your opinions, making you easily confused. You'll likely have trouble grasping the spiritual side of things and seeing the link between your inner and outer selves. This leads to a lack of empathy for those around you, which clouds your vision and makes it difficult to envision a life you want to live.

So, how do you know you are in the process of third eye activation? You get a feeling. You're strolling through the woods and have the option of taking one of two paths. Your gut tells you that you're on the correct track. Or maybe your phone is ringing, and you know who the caller is without looking. You meet someone and your intuition tells you they aren't trustworthy. Intuition is a powerful tool. All of these scenarios have something to do with the third eye. You will undoubtedly come into contact with similar situations as you progress spiritually. The more your third eye opens, the more intuitive you become.

It takes time to open the third eye. At the beginning, you might feel a certain amount of pressure between your eyes, where the third eye is located. Don't let this worry you, because it isn't permanent.

Your dreams will become more vivid, and you may remember them better while your third eye is in the process of activation. You might also begin to have a lot of déjà vu experiences. You'll likely begin to feel more creative, will feel an urge to get out in nature, and will begin to notice your sense of intuition becoming sharper by the day.

These are just some of the phenomena you may experience after activating your *Ajna Chakra*. In the next chapter, we will explore the history of the third eye to better understand its role in religious, spiritual, and philosophical lines of thought.

Chapter 2: History of the Third Eye

Henri Ellenberger (1970) explored early Western contributions to the field of psychiatry in his mammoth work, *The Discovery of the Unconscious*. The title emphasizes that, despite the fact that the unconscious is always present, we are mostly ignorant of its functions and presence.

The psychoanalysts Sigmund Freud and Carl Jung stand out in the twentieth century. Their writings are frequently discussed and have many websites dedicated to them. The notions of the ego, id, and superego were introduced by Sigmund Freud, the founder of psychoanalysis. He developed these concepts along with the conscious-unconscious dichotomy. Jung's method is significantly more complicated, with notions like the collective unconscious and archetypes introduced.

In his early 19th-century work, *The World as Will and Representation* (1819), Arthur Schopenhauer associated the human will with the unconscious. In essence, Schopenhauer maintained that man's irrationality is mostly attributable to the unconscious's dark, deeply concealed energies. These are impacts that the average person isn't even aware of. Carl Gustav Carus (1846) proposed the first notion of the unconscious in his work *Psyche*. Dessoir (1890) argued for the twin ego in his reflections on the human psyche. There is an above consciousness and an under-consciousness, according to his definition (presumably unconscious). Even more intriguing is Theodore Flournoy's (1899) investigation, which looked into the unconscious origins of communications that were previously supposed to come from the spiritual realm. Theodor Lipps (1896) proposed that past images are active in oneself without one being conscious of their presence and activity. He is the one who coined the analogy of the unconscious as submerged mountains and awareness as their exposed peaks. Using this parallel, he argued that the unconscious is a psychological issue.

Rene Descarte highlighted the importance of the pineal gland in his letters, and his very first work, the *Treatise of Man* (1633), and his last book, *The Passions of the Soul* (1649). The pineal gland, he believed, is the very seat of the human soul because of its central location in the brain.

The pineal gland is located in the center of the brain, between the two hemispheres. The pineal gland is mostly composed of pinealocytes, which generate melatonin, and glial cells, a kind of brain cell that supports neurons.

In *The Passions of the Soul*, Descartes splits man into a body and a soul, underlining that the soul is linked to the entire body via a little gland located in the midst of the brain's substance. Descartes valued the gland because he believed it was the only part of the brain that evolved as a single unit rather than as half of a pair.

The pineal gland, in fact, has been a component of human civilization since antiquity. The extensive writings of Galen (c.130 AD - c.210 AD), the Greek medical practitioner and philosopher who spent most of his time in Rome and whose system influenced medical thought until the seventeenth century, includes the first characterization of the pineal gland and ideas regarding its activities.

Galen described the pineal gland in the eighth volume of his anatomical treatise on the efficacy of the parts of the body. He mentioned that it takes its name from the nuts found in stone pine cones. He called it a gland because of its appearance and stated that it serves the same role as all other glands in the body: To assist blood vessels.

The following two points should be kept in mind in order to grasp the rest of Galen's exposition. To begin with, his nomenclature differed from ours. He considered the brain's lateral ventricles to be one paired ventricle, which he dubbed the anterior ventricle. As a result, he named the third ventricle the intermediate ventricle and the fourth ventricle the posterior ventricle. Second, he believed these ventricles were filled with "psychological pneuma," a delicate, volatile, airy or vaporous fluid he referred to as "the soul's first instrument."

Galen went to tremendous lengths to rebut a viewpoint that appeared to be popular at the time, but whose authors or champions he did not name. According to them, the pineal gland governs the flow of psychic pneuma in the canal between the brain's middle and posterior ventricles, much as the pylorus regulates food passage from the esophagus to the stomach. Galen criticized this hypothesis because the pineal gland is connected to the outside of the brain and cannot move on its own. He stated that the "worm-like appendage" [epiphysis or apophysis] of the cerebellum (now known as the vermis superior cerebelli) is significantly more capable of performing this role.

Galen's opinions were frequently broadened or amended, even though he was the undisputed medical authority until the seventeenth century. The inclusion of a ventricular localization theory of psychological abilities to Galen's explanation of the brain is an early example of this occurrence. Posidonius of Byzantium (end of the fourth century CE) provided the earliest hypothesis of this type, claiming that imagination is attributable to the forepart of the brain, reason to the middle ventricle, and memory to the hind part of the brain. Nemesius of Emesa, a few decades later, was more explicit, claiming that the front ventricle is the organ of imagination, the middle ventricle is the organ of reason, and the posterior ventricle is the organ of memory. Until the middle of the sixteenth century, the latter notion was virtually universally accepted, but there were many variations.

According to Descartes, the body is nothing more than a statue or machine that God created. The operation of these bodies may be completely explained in mechanical terms. Descartes attempted to demonstrate that such a structural account can explain much more than one might expect because it can explain food absorption, heart and arterial function, nourishment and growth of the limbs, respiration, waking and sleeping, and the reception of light, sounds, smells, tastes, heat, and other such qualities by the external sense organs. So, he did not consider our bodies to be anything more than vehicles for different activities.

Descartes emphasized that the soul is joined to the entire body just before mentioning the pineal gland for the first time: "We must recognize that the soul is truly joined to the entire body, and that we cannot properly say that it exists in any one part of the body to the exclusion of the others," he said. Because the organs are so closely interconnected to one another that removing any one of them renders the entire body faulty, the body is a unity that is in some ways indivisible. And the soul is of such a character that it has no relation to extension, dimensions, or other attributes of the stuff that makes up the body: it is only linked to the entire collection of organs. This is evident in our incapacity to comprehend a half or a third of a soul, or the space that a soul takes up. The soul does not shrink when a part of the body is removed, but it does become fully distinct from the body when the body's organs are dismantled. Despite the fact that the soul is connected to the entire body, there is one portion of the body where it performs its activities more specifically than the rest. The heart or the entire brain are not the parts of the body where the soul directly performs its tasks. It is the innermost region of the brain, which is a tiny gland suspended above the pathway through which the spirits of the brain's anterior cavities connect with those of the brain's posterior cavities. The tiniest motions of this gland can have a significant impact on the route of these spirits, and any change in the path of the spirits, no matter how minor, can have a significant impact on the gland's motions.

He went on to say that he believes our views about gravity are formed from our understanding of the soul. Descartes' account included the pineal gland, which was involved in sensation, imagination, memory, and the causality of bodily motions.

Until the second part of the nineteenth century, little progress was achieved in scientific research of the pineal gland. At this point, various researchers proposed that the pineal gland is a phylogenetic relic, a remnant of a dorsal third eye. This thesis, in a modified version, is still widely accepted today. Scientists also came to the conclusion that the pineal gland is an endocrine organ. In the twentieth century, this hypothesis was proven without a shadow of a doubt. Melatonin, a hormone released by the pineal gland, was discovered in 1958. Melatonin is secreted in a diurnal pattern, which is intriguing given that the pineal gland is thought to be a vestige of the third eye. In the 1990s, melatonin was lauded as a "miracle medication" and went on to become one of the most popular health supplements. Philosophers of science gave considerable thought to the history of pineal gland research in the twentieth century, although this exploration was short-lived.

The pineal gland maintained its lofty status in the domain of pseudo-science as philosophy downgraded it to simply another portion of the brain and science analyzed it as one endocrine gland among many. Madame Blavatsky, the creator of theosophy, linked the "third eye" discovered by comparative anatomists of her time to the "eye of Shiva" of "the Hindu mystics," concluding that modern man's pineal body is an atrophied residue of this "organ of spiritual vision". This notion is still widely accepted in spiritual circles today.

The third eye's reputation extends far beyond its material characteristics, and its spiritual meanings become transcendent. Telepathy, divination, lucid dreaming, and astral projection are all possible with a developed third eye.

Because the third eye is the foundation of all psychic abilities, no spiritual teaching is complete without doctrines on it. No spiritual connections are conceivable without a strong mastery of this Chakra, without which we are condemned to a prosaic third-dimensional existence. Certain pineal exercises were devised in ancient Egypt, when psychic development was at its peak.

I know this was a little heavy—but context helps you understand that you are not alone in your quest for divinity. Others have come before you, researched and debated and laid the groundwork so that you can take your steps into actualization of your true being. Let us now move on and look at the other chakras of our body, and what we can do to keep them in balance.

Chapter 3: The Other Chakras

If you're just getting started, learning how to open your third eye isn't something you can do in an afternoon—it takes a lot of time and effort, including laying a solid foundation. It's crucial to create the energetic foundation of the first five chakras, starting at the root, before opening the third eye. Trying to awaken the third eye before working with the bottom five chakras is like learning to jump before being able to stand on two feet. In fact, prematurely activating the third eye can cause a spiritual crisis, which is commonly misinterpreted as psychosis.

To put it another way, if opening the third eye is your ultimate goal, it's time to start clearing and balancing the other chakras. After you've done that, you can begin to work on opening the sixth chakra. But keep in mind that this takes time, so be patient with yourself as you go.

So, what are the other *chakras* you need to focus on?

The Root Chakra

The base of the spine, the pelvic floor, and the first three vertebrae are all connected to the *root chakra*. Consider your *root chakra* (also known as *Muladhara* in Sanskrit) to be the foundation of your house (in this case, the house is your body).

It's solid, steady, and supportive when it's in balance. As a result, it's in charge of your sense of safety and survival. It's also linked to whatever you use to ground yourself, such as essential necessities like food, water, shelter, and safety, as well as deeper emotional needs like feeling safe. As you may be aware, when these requirements are addressed, you are less likely to be anxious or concerned.

Blockages can cause a number of diseases, including anxiety problems, stress, and nightmares, according to believers. Physically, the first *chakra* is linked to colon, bladder, and elimination disorders, as well as lower back, leg, and foot disorders.

The *root chakra*, like any other *chakra*, can be underactive or overactive. If it's underactive, it might be closed or blocked in some way, or it may not be spinning effectively. As a result, we may feel worried, uneasy, and unsafe, or in other words, ungrounded. When the energies are overactive, it's as if they're working overtime and become unhealthily linked to the physical and material world. An overactive root chakra manifests itself in overindulging in bodily pleasures such as food or sex, becoming overly connected to money, and an obsession with feeling safe.

Exercise to balance your root chakra: Mountain Pose (*Tadasana*)

Mountain Pose, the cornerstone of all standing poses, is an excellent resting pose, or aid for improving posture.

Step 1: Stand with your big toes touching and your heels marginally apart (so that your second toes are parallel). Lift and stretch your toes and balls of your feet before gently laying them on the floor. Rock from side to side and back and forth. Gradually bring your swaying to a halt by balancing your weight evenly on both feet.

Step 2: Tighten your thigh muscles and elevate your knee caps without clenching your lower stomach. Lift your ankles to strengthen your inner arches, then visualize a line of energy running from your inner thighs to your groin, then through your torso, neck, and head, and out the crown of your head. Then, with a slightly inward turn of the upper thighs, lift your pubis toward the navel and extend your tailbone toward the floor.

Step 3: Push your shoulder blades into your back, then widen and release them down your spine. Lift the top of your sternum straight toward the ceiling without forcing your lower front ribs forward. Increase the width of your collarbones. Place your arms alongside your torso.

Step 4: With the bottom of your chin parallel to the floor, throat soft, and tongue wide and flat on the floor of your mouth, balance the top of your head directly over the center of your pelvis. Relax your gaze.

Step 5: Tadasana is the most common starting point for all standing poses. However, practicing Tadasana as a stand-alone pose is beneficial. Hold the stance for 30 seconds to 1 minute, breathing normally.

The Sacral Chakra

This *chakra* is located above the pubic bone and just below the navel. *Svadhisthana,* or the second *chakra,* is the creative and sexual energy center of the body, and it holds our emotions, passions, and pleasures—the things that emotionally satiate and bring us delight. You'll probably feel wonderful when your *sacral chakra* is aligned. This means that you feel outgoing, enthusiastic, and successful, and you exude feelings of well-being, affluence, pleasure, and joy.

Your *sacral chakra* may be misaligned if you're feeling uninspired artistically or have emotional instability. Similarly, this can be linked to physical sexual dysfunction, as well as fear of change, despair, or addiction-like behaviors. You may have poor libido, a lack of joy in life, or hormone and fertility concerns if your *sacral chakra* is underactive. When you're overactive, you're more likely to develop addictions, sexual or otherwise, and you're more likely to have a lot of emotional ups and downs.

Exercise to balance your sacral chakra: Goddess Pose

Goddess posture encourages us to connect with our inner divine feminine, harmonizing our strength and determination with profound inner wisdom.

Precaution: If you have an injury to your hips, legs, ankles, or feet, this position may not be suitable for you.

Step 1: Take a big, open step with your right foot toward the rear of your mat, starting in Tadasana (a comfortable standing posture with your feet hip width and parallel at the top of your mat). Make a 45-degree angle with your toes. Advanced practitioners might start to align their heels with their toes (and the long edge of the mat).

Step 2: Bend your knees so they drop directly over your ankles, moving the knees toward each foot's second and third toes. While engaging the core, lower the tailbone and sink the hips. Draw the navel in closer to the spine by lifting the pelvic floor.

Step 3: Spread your fingers and extend your arms forward, allowing your pinky fingers to spin inward. Your shoulder blades might glide down your back when your hands face each other.

Step 4: Lengthen the spine by lifting through the heart center and bringing the floating ribs in.

Step 5: Breathe deeply for five minutes, with your exhalation slightly longer than your inhalation.

For variations, put your hands to your thighs and twist. Inhale deeply into your stomach. Exhale and bring your right shoulder into the center of your body, with your eyes passing over your left shoulder. Inhale into your belly button and exhale through your center. Then exhale and gaze over your right shoulder, dropping your left shoulder into the center.

The Solar Plexus Chakra

This *chakra* is said to control everything metabolic, digestive, and stomach-related from the navel to approximately the ribcage. The third *chakra*, which has the Sanskrit name *Manipura*, which means "lustrous gem," is thought to be your source of personal power. Individual willpower, personal power, and devotion are controlled by this chakra.

You may experience low self-esteem, difficulties making decisions, and anger or control issues if it is obstructed. It's not only about feeling horrible about yourself; it may also lead to outward displays of apathy, procrastination, or the feeling of being easily exploited. You may also experience a gut ache of some sort, such as digestive problems or gas.

We will battle with self-doubt and being our highest, most true selves if the solar plexus chakra is obstructed. On the other hand, indicators of an overactive solar plexus include a rampant ego, which manifests as power-hungry and egotistical conduct, as well as manic behavior and hyperactive energy.

Exercise to balance your solar plexus chakra: Boat Pose (*Navasana*)

The Boat pose requires you to coordinate the activity of your limbs and torso while also strengthening your spine. It will educate you about your breathing, attention span, emotions, and perhaps your own personality. Even a simple stance like Navasana can eventually enter your Self—your innermost core— beyond the muscles, nerves, joints, and organs. The stomach moves toward the spine, the spine moves forth to support the front of the trunk, and shoulder blades go down and in toward the chest while the chest expands, and the arms and legs remain firm. Full Boat Pose will leave you feeling strong and supple, as well as psychologically and emotionally stable, due to the integration of all of your bodily parts.

Step 1: Begin by bending your knees and placing your feet flat on the floor in a seated position. Raise your feet from the ground. At the start, keep your knees bent. Make sure your shins are parallel to the ground. This is the half-boat position. Although your torso will naturally fall back, do not allow your spine to round.

Step 2: If you can do so without jeopardizing your upper body's integrity, straighten your legs to a 45-degree angle. Maintain a V shape with your legs by keeping your torso as erect as possible.

Step 3: With your palms turned up, roll your shoulders back and straighten your arms nearly parallel to the floor. To keep balance, concentrate on elevating your chest.

Step 4: Take at least five deep breaths.

Step 5: Exhale and release your legs. Then take a deep breath and sit up.

The Heart Chakra

The heart, the thymus gland (which plays a critical part in your endocrine and lymphatic systems), the lungs, and the breasts are all encapsulated by the heart chakra, which is located in the center of the chest. The fourth (or Anahata) chakra signifies the meeting of the physical and spiritual worlds as the center chakra. And, as the name suggests, it's all about love. It's a spiritual chakra that governs forgiveness, service, and spiritual awareness. Love and compassion are said to flow readily when your heart chakra is connected and balanced, both in terms of sending it out and receiving it.

Grief, rage, envy, fear of rejection, and animosity toward yourself and others can all result from a closed heart chakra. We may become emotionally closed off and find it difficult to forgive and let go of past hurts when this chakra is underactive. As a result, it may become difficult to offer and receive love, negatively impacting our relationships.

We may become excessively affectionate if this chakra is overactive. On the surface, this may not appear to be a problem, but it is frequently a cover for codependency.

Exercise to balance your heart chakra: Upward Dog

Urdhva Mukha Svanasana (Upward-Facing Dog) is an energizing backbend that strengthens the arms and legs while opening the chest and shoulders. It's the foundation of Sun Salutations and is used frequently in flow sessions in between other postures. When practicing Up Dog, it's crucial to link breath to movement since the breath animates and illuminates the posture while also opening the heart.

Step 1: Begin by lying face-down on the floor with your legs stretched a few inches apart behind you. The tops of your feet should rest on the mat; do not bury your toes into the mat, as this will cause your spine to crunch.

Step 2: Place your hands on the floor next to your lower ribs, beside your body. Hug your elbows tight to your ribcage and point your fingertips to the top of the mat.

Step 3: Inhale as you firmly press your hands into the ground. Straighten your arms and lift your torso and legs off the floor a few inches. *Chaturanga* is another way to get into the position (low plank). Draw your body forward from *Chaturanga* by squeezing through your palms and rolling over your toes. Straighten your arms and align your shoulders directly over your wrists.

Step 4: Firmly press down on the tops of your feet. Keep your thighs elevated off the floor by firmly engaging your leg muscles. Maintain a parallel relationship between your elbows and your body. Lift your chest toward the sky and drop your shoulders away from your ears.

Step 5: Draw your shoulders back and your heart forward, but don't make your neck crunch. Tilt your head toward the sky if your neck is flexible. Otherwise, maintain a neutral head position and a straightforward stare. Your thighs should be strong and inwardly inclined. Your arms should also be solid and slightly turned forward, with the creases of each elbow facing forward.

Step 6: Straighten your arms only as far as your body will allow. As your practice progresses, deepen the stretch while avoiding straining to reach a deeper backbend.

Step 7: Activate your shoulder blades by pressing them into your upper back. Maintain a tight grip on your sides using your elbows. Lift your heart and broaden your collarbones. Glide your shoulders back and away from your ears. The length of the backbend should be uniformly distributed throughout your entire spine.

Step 8: Maintain the position for up to 30 seconds. Exhale as you lower your torso and forehead to the mat to release.

The Throat Chakra

The thyroid, parathyroid, jaw, neck, mouth, tongue, and larynx are all connected to the *throat chakra* anatomically. Your fifth *chakra*, which is all about speaking your inner truth—or, more specifically, ensuring that your inner truths are appropriately communicated—is likely well-balanced if you have no trouble expressing yourself. The throat chakra, also known as *Vishuddha* in Sanskrit, is in charge of all communication. It's the first of three chakras that are completely spiritual (as opposed to the lower ones, which manifest themselves in a more physical way). You can fully listen as well as speak and express yourself clearly when this chakra is balanced.

When the *throat chakra* is underactive, it might be difficult to properly express oneself. You might physically swallow your words, and with them, your actual feelings. In addition to having difficulty stating your truth, you may struggle to pay attention and stay focused, or you may be afraid of being judged by others, which can make it even more difficult to be yourself. A sore throat, thyroid difficulties, neck and shoulder discomfort, or tension headaches are all symptoms of a blockage.

Talking too much, being extremely dominant in conversations, and being overly critical or judgmental of others are all signs of an overworked throat chakra.

Exercise to balance your throat chakra: Fish Pose

The back-bending yoga posture Fish Pose (*Matsyasana*) expands the chest, neck, and abdomen. It's often used as a counterpose to Shoulder Stand (*Sarvangasana*) since it relieves pressure on the neck and spine, but it's also a deep stretch with numerous advantages.

Step 1: Start by lying down on your back with your legs outstretched and with your arms resting beside your body, palms down.

Step 2: To produce an arch in your upper back, press your forearms and elbows into the ground and lift your chest. Raise your upper chest and shoulder blades off the floor. Tilt your head backward and touch the floor with the crown of your head.

Step 3: Continue to apply pressure with your hands and forearms. There should be hardly any pressure exerted on your head. Through your heels, push outward.

Step 4: Take five deep breaths and hold. To come out of the posture, lift your head off the floor by pressing strongly through your forearms. Then, as you drop your torso and head to the ground, exhale. Draw your knees into your chest for a few breaths in Knees-to-Chest Pose (*Apanasana*), then stretch your legs and rest.

The Crown Chakra

Finally, before going on to the *third eye chakra*, we have the *crown chakra*. The *crown chakra*, also known as *Sahasrara* or the "thousand petal lotus" *chakra* in Sanskrit, is the center of enlightenment and our spiritual link to our greater selves, the greater selves of others, and ultimately the divine. When this chakra is in balance, your spiritual awakenings are considered to be along the lines of pure consciousness—undivided and all-encompassing. Basically, you're bigger than your physical being, and you're also a part of a larger world. We may feel indifferent, almost energetically numb, and disconnected if we have an underactive *crown chakra*, resulting in a lack of direction and purpose in life.

The *crown chakra*, unlike the other *chakras*, is typically only fully opened through specialized yogic or meditation exercises, or at specified times—it is not a skill set you can call upon at any time. You might be able to acquire a taste of it by engaging in everyday activities such as meditation, prayer, and periods of stillness. An underactive *crown chakra* may lead to confusion, a desire to oversleep, and general apathy with life.

A yearning for material possessions that never seems to be satiated is a common symptom of a hyperactive *crown chakra*. Greed, superficiality, and arrogance frequently lead to a loss of connection with others and the cosmos.

Exercise to balance your crown chakra: Headstand

The king of all *asanas*, *Sirsasana* or Headstand Pose, is a pose that requires equilibrium on the head/crown. This is a difficult yoga pose that should only be done with the help of a yoga instructor. Because of its numerous health benefits, this asana is quite popular. It improves blood circulation and ensures that enough well-oxygenated blood reaches the brain.

Step 1: Kneel on the ground to get started. If you want to be more comfortable, use a yoga mat. Bring your knees and ankles together, and point your feet in the same direction as your legs. With your big toes touching, the bottoms of your feet should face upward.

Step 2: Sit back on your legs and exhale. Your thighs will lie on your calves while your buttocks rest on your heels. Place your hands on your thighs and move your pelvis back and forth until a feeling of satisfaction comes over you. You are now in *vajrasana*.

Step 3: Bend forward with interlocked fingers and folded forearms on the ground. The head, hands, and feet should create a triangle on the floor.

Step 4: Place the crown of the head between the clasped fingers. Straighten your knees and glutes by raising them off the floor. Slowly approach the trunk with your feet.

Step 5: Bend your knees, keeping your heels close to your buttocks, and slowly straighten your hips until your thighs are perpendicular to the floor. Slowly straighten the knees and calves until the entire body is erect and the feet are relaxed.

Step 6: Maintain your body's balance for a few seconds or as long as you feel comfortable. Advanced yoga practitioners should begin with one minute and gradually increase to at least five minutes. Concentrate on your breathing and the top of your head.

Step 7: Retrace your steps in the other direction when you wish to return from the pose. Fold your legs and return your thighs to a perpendicular position slowly.

Step 8: Drop your legs to the ground gradually. Sit in *Shishuasana* (Child Pose) for a while to regain your equilibrium after being inverted.

Step 9: Relax and breathe out.

Chapter 4: The Sixth Chakra

The third eye is a *chakra*, or energy point. It is related to the pineal and pituitary glands on the brain and is placed on the forehead between the brows, though it is not a physical construct. The *chakra* system functions similarly to the organ system of the subtle (or energetic) body, with each *chakra* serving a distinct role or purpose. Our inner clarity, intuition, and foresight are all accessed through the third eye. It enables us to look beyond what is physically accessible in the present time.

Confusion, doubt, cynicism, envy, and pessimism are all thought to be symptoms of a blocked third eye, or *ajna chakra*. The highest source of ethereal energy can enter through an open and lively third eye. The third eye sees the genuine world — a unified whole with an unwavering link to spirit — while the physical eyes see the limited apparent reality. Clarity, concentration, perspicuity, bliss, intuition, decisiveness, and insight are just a few of the benefits and abilities that the third eye provides. Lucid dreaming, astral projection, sleep quality, heightened creativity, and aura viewing have all been connected to the third eye. Though the first third eye seekers were monks and enlightened beings, these activities are good for those of us who live busy modern lives, racing to and from work and play dates while wanting a little more calm and presence.

Some of us may have even experienced third eye awakening in our daily lives! When a person is intensely concentrated on their work, they may experience third eye activation. When an athlete is very focused on their practice, continuously thinking about the game and how they might play it better, they acquire an intuitive feel of where an airborne ball will land. A top athlete doesn't need an analyst to tell them what's going to happen next; they intuitively know what will happen. Even a person who is completely focused on their profession can predict how a client will react to a particular offering or event. The increased alpha wave emissions assist them in predicting what may occur in the near future in relation to the field on which they are intensely focused.

However, if you've never felt a twinge of energy between your brows, seen auras, or received an intuitive hit, don't worry. You do not need to be born with special abilities to use your third sight. Its superpowers are accessible to everyone willing to put in the effort. Just as building physical muscles necessitates a targeted workout program, developing the Third Eye necessitates a systematic approach and constant practice. Though it's certainly simpler to get toned arms than it is to become a full-fledged intuitive, we can all benefit from consistently exercising this energy channel.

When working at full capacity, the third eye can assist you in seeing clearly, clearing mental blocks, and improving mental flexibility. In fact, in many cultures, the third eye is regarded as the most significant sense, and activating it is considered to be of utmost importance. While the third eye has the advantage of connecting us to our gut instincts and allowing us to operate one step ahead of our five basic senses, it is usually closed. That's when meditation's advantages come into play. Meditation is the simplest and most effective approach to awaken, vitalize, and activate your third eye.

It's best to start with an activation exercise when opening your third eye. Begin by thanking your third eye for your inherent intuitive abilities as well as your rootedness through the pineal gland's circadian rhythms. The pineal gland connects the endocrine and neurological systems by converting nerve signals from the peripheral nervous system's sympathetic system into hormone signals. Calcium deposits build up in the pineal over time, calcifying it and rendering it worthless.

Fluoride also calcifies the gland, making it less effective in balancing the complete hormonal processes throughout the body, according to a study conducted by British scientist Jennifer Luke in the 1990s. Fluoride is currently found in a wide range of products, including our drinking water, food, soft drinks, and even toothpaste. Fluoride is a common, plentiful, and natural element, but it may also be synthesized in the lab. Excess sugar, food additives, and sweeteners in your diet, as well as excessive cellphone use, all contribute to calcification.

Before beginning any new nutrition regimen, always see a trained Nutritional Therapist to ensure that you are doing what is best for you and that you are not depleting your body of essential nutrients.

The food you eat can help you open your third eye chakra. Raw cacao, goji berries, garlic, lemon, watermelon, star anise, honey, coconut oil, hemp seeds, cilantro, ginseng, and vitamin D3 are just a few foods that are said to help to strengthen and detoxify the third eye.

Foods to avoid because they cause the pineal gland to calcify:

- Calcium phosphate buildup in our bodies can be caused by consuming too much calcium from processed foods or taking too many calcium supplements. To avoid acquiring an excessive amount of this substance in your diet, read the ingredients on items.

- Tap Water: In addition to fluoride, the water supply contains calcified compounds that might be harmful, therefore drink bottled or filtered water instead whenever possible.

- Pesticides: The pineal gland can be poisoned by chemical pesticides found in meats and vegetables. To limit the number of pesticides in your diet, choose organic foods.

- Also, keep an eye out for products containing Propylene Glycol, Paraffin, Mineral Oil, Butylene Glycol, Isopropyl Alcohol, and Petrolatum. If a food item contains any of these ingredients, it's time to hunt for an alternative. Instead, seek out natural plant oils, which provide ample nutrients while posing no risk to your health.

- Sugar, Caffeine, Alcohol, and Tobacco (S.C.A.T.) These drugs deplete the body's vitality and cause pollutants to accumulate. Cutting them out of your life for at least two months can result in an increase in brain activity as well as pineal gland activity.

Natural food items that will help in activating your third eye include:

- Activator X: This is a detoxifier made up of vitamin K1/K2, which can be coupled with vitamin D3 and A. This detoxifier can aid in the restoration of enzymatic balance, allowing calcium to leave the arteries and enter the bones, where it can be appropriately utilized.

- Chocolate in its natural state: Raw cacao is abundant in antioxidants, which can aid in stimulating and cleaning the pineal gland—finally, an excuse to consume chocolate!

- Garlic cloves: Garlic is a powerful natural cleanser that can also help remove calcium in the body. Consume half to two bulbs per day—eating them fresh or soaking them in fresh lemon juice or apple cider vinegar can help to mask the odor.

- Distilled water: Toxins that may be damaging the pineal gland can be flushed away by drinking plenty of flucride-free water.

- Citric acid: On an empty stomach, raw lemon can aid in detoxing the pineal gland. It's best to combine this with spring water to avoid putting too much acid on your teeth.

- Apple Cider Vinegar: Because of the malic acid it contains, adding apple cider vinegar to your meals is an excellent approach to detoxify the pineal gland.

- Virgin coconut oil: Coconut oil nourishes the whole human body, but it may provide the greatest impact in terms of brain revitalization and pineal gland detoxification. In the brain, this oil repairs neurons and promotes nerve function.

We can experience vivid visions and deep relaxation when the pineal gland is aroused. Inversions are particularly beneficial because they enhance blood flow to the pineal gland when upside down, and they have numerous other health benefits such as improving sleep quality.

Meditation will greatly wake up your pineal gland, particularly if you practice it outside in the morning while the sun is rising, or at dusk.

It takes dedication and work to reawaken your pineal gland and enjoy its full potential. Be patient with yourself and realize that anything that occurs organically takes longer, but the health advantages are well worth the wait! Meditation aids in the removal of negative poisons from the body, the channeling of energies, and the improvement of concentration. Meditation can also help you become more self-aware, activate your ajna chakra, shift your state of consciousness to higher states with each session, and remove anxiety and worries.

Third eye meditation, like any other form of meditation, necessitates that you remain in a peaceful setting. To begin, take a seat in a comfortable position on a chair or on the floor. Maintain a straight spine, relaxed shoulders, and place your hands on your knees. The jaw, stomach, and face should all be completely relaxed and open to positive energy.

Begin by softly bringing your index and middle fingers together and closing your eyes. After that, gently take a deep breath. Inhale via your nose and exhale through your mouth. Try to glance up at the third eye, which is placed just between your brows, with your eyes closed. You can also use your fingertips to pinpoint the exact location.

Next, take a few deep breaths and direct your attention to this point. Continue doing so while visualizing a white or bluish-white light surrounding you. As you do so, you will enter a transcendental state of healing, in which your attention will be at its peak.

Hold this position for 10-20 minutes. Relaxing music can help you channel your concentration even further. After that, exhale deeply and bring your palms together in front of your heart before returning to the starting posture. Blink your eyes open and hold this position for a second or two before returning to your normal routine. This simple action can perform miracles and repair your chakras if done every day, either in the morning or before retiring for the night.

Alternate Nostril Breathing

Nadis are delicate energy lines that can become obstructed for a variety of reasons. The *Nadi Shodhan pranayama* is a breathing method that aids in the clearing of these clogged energy pathways, hence soothing the mind. Anulom Vilom pranayama is another name for this practice. Stress, toxicity in the physical body, physical and mental trauma, and an unhealthy lifestyle can cause *Nadis* to become obstructed.

Three of the most important nadis in the human body are *Ida, Pingala*, and *Sushumna*.

Cold, depression, low mental energy, sluggish digestion, and a blocked left nostril are all symptoms of the *Ida nadi* not functioning properly or being obstructed. Heat, irritability, itching, dry skin and throat, increased appetite, excessive physical or sexual energy, and a clogged right nostril are all symptoms of the *Pingala nadi* not functioning properly or being obstructed.

The *Nadi Shodhan pranayama* (alternate nostril breathing) helps to calm the mind and prepare it for meditation. It helps to keep the mind quiet, cheerful, and serene if you practice it for just a few minutes each day. It aids in the release of tension and tiredness.

Step 1: Sit comfortably with your shoulders relaxed and your spine erect. Maintain a soft smile on your lips.

Step 2: Place your left hand on your left knee with palms facing up or in Chin Mudra (thumb and index finger gently touching at the tips).

Step 3: Between the brows, place the tips of the index and middle fingers of the right hand, the ring and little fingers on the left nostril, and the thumb on the right nostril. The left nostril will be opened or closed using the ring and little fingers, while the right nostril will be opened or closed with the thumb.

Step 4: Breathe out slowly through the left nostril while pressing your thumb on the right nostril.

Step 5: Inhale deeply through the left nostril, then gently press the left nostril with the ring and little fingers. Breathe out from the right nostril after removing the right thumb from the right nostril.

Step 6: Inhale via your right nostril and exhale via your left. One round of Nadi Shodhan pranayama has been completed. Continue to breathe in and out through alternate nostrils.

Step 7: Complete 9 rounds by breathing through both nostrils alternately. Remember to breathe in through the same nostril you exhaled from after each exhalation. Close your eyes and continue to take long, deep, smooth breaths without exerting any energy or effort.

After conducting *Nadi Shodhan pranayama*, it's a good idea to do a short meditation. As part of the *Padma Sadhana* routine, this breathing technique can be used.

Apart from opening your third eye, *Nadi Shodhan Pranayama* has several major benefits:

- Excellent technique for calming and centering the mind.

- Our minds have a tendency to dwell on the past, regretting or glorifying it, and worrying about the future. The pranayama of Nadi Shodhan assists in bringing the mind back to the present moment.

- Many circulatory and respiratory issues can be improved with this technique.

- Effectively relieves accumulated stress in the mind and body and aids relaxation.

- Helps to balance the left and right hemispheres of the brain, which correspond to our intellectual and emotional sides.

- Purifies and balances the nadis, or subtle energy channels, allowing prana (life force) to circulate freely throughout the body.

- Helps you to maintain a comfortable body temperature.

To See the Unseen

Many people are taught from a young age not to trust their own instincts. This could have come from your parents or friends convincing you that your senses were not valid, causing you to distrust yourself. As a survival technique, mistreated children will disconnect from their lower *chakras*, causing their higher chakras to overdevelop. An imbalance between the lower and upper chakras can drive these children to use imagination and visualization to escape reality. People will become dreamers rather than doers as a result of this in the long run. To have a well-functioning *Ajna*, one needs to first have balanced lower *chakras* as an anchor.

Our perspective is likewise influenced by the *Ajna*. Perceptions are something we all share. Our perception is shaped by our upbringing, surroundings, and beliefs. We can get into problems if perception is misinterpreted for intuition. Reality isn't always what we think it is. To bring the *Ajna* into balance, we must question our perceptions and always seek reality, no matter how unpleasant it may be.

It takes time to strengthen and balance the *Ajna*. To function properly, the Ajna needs daily meditation. The results will be subtle, and if they aren't observed, they can easily go unnoticed. When it comes to regaining *Ajna* equilibrium, it's critical to learn to trust your intuition and what you perceive in meditation. Understand the distinctions between ideas, perceptions, and intuition. Intuition is a natural process that has no preferences. The *Ajna* is a wonderful gift, and having one that is completely functional will allow you to achieve your maximum potential.

An incredible meditation for the *Ajna* is called "To See the Unseen." It strengthens your intuition by working on the sixth chakra.

Step 1: Sit in a comfortable position with your right arm extended in front of you, parallel to the floor, and your elbow straight but not locked. The right hand's palm is pointing up and cupped slightly, as if catching rain.

Step 2: With the elbow at the side and forearm facing out, the left hand is in *Surya Mudra* (ring finger contacting thumb).

Step 3: Close your eyes and concentrate on the chin's tip.

Step 4: Press the tip of your tongue firmly onto the palate behind your teeth.

Step 5: Mentally repeat "*Wahe Guru*."

Step 6: Take a long, deep breath. Repeat this 11 times.

To finish, create panther claws (bend the fingers into the mounds of the hand). Inhale and turn to the left, then exhale and return to the center. Then inhale and turn to the right, then exhale and return to the center.

Cross Heart Kirtan Kriya

Step 1: Sit with a straight spine in *Sukhasana* (Easy Pose). Close your eyes for a moment and then slowly open them. Focus your attention on the tip of your nose. Meditating here can help quiet a chattering mind.

Step 2: In front of the chest, cross the forearms. Prepare to use the mantra *Saa-Taa-Naa-Maa* in your work. Infinity is denoted by *Saa*, life is *Taa*, and transformation is *Naa*. *Maa* is the goddess of rebirth.

Step 3: Begin chanting, *saa – taa – naa – maa,* while playing the fingers in the following manner:

Touch the tips of your thumbs to the tips of your index fingers *(saa)*.

Touch the tips of the thumbs to the middle fingers *(taa)*.

Touch the tips of your thumbs to your ring fingers *(naa)*.

Touch the tips of your thumbs to your pinkie fingers *(maa)*.

Step 4: Repeat for several minutes. To finish, take a deep breath, hold it, close your eyes, and become perfectly still. Allow yourself to unwind. The hemispheres will be in balance, and there will be a new sense of serenity.

The Archer Pose

Akarna Dhanurasana literally translates to "Toward-the-Ear Bow Pose," but it's popularly known as "*Archer Pose*" because it looks like an archer about to release her arrow. It takes talent and patience to observe yourself in this way. The spiritual dimension of the practice will always be elusive if the archer is just concerned with pulling the bowstring and striking the target, or if the yogi is just concerned with getting into the physical shape of the position.

Physical ability and technique are important, but you must eventually let go of your obsession with performing a set of actions. You can let go of superfluous effort and fully occupy and express the limitless present by cultivating body steadiness, eye relaxation, and complete surrender to the breath. *Akarna Dhanurasana*, like archery, requires both strength and flexibility on a physical level. The exercises in the following sequence are designed to help you gain strength in your arms and torso as well as flexibility in your legs and hips.

Step 1: Sit on the mat with your back straight, your legs out in front of you, and your palms on your knees.

Step 2: Bend your right leg such that the sole of your right foot touches the left thigh.

Step 3: Bend forward and grab your left hand with your left big toe as you inhale. Your other hand should be resting on your right knee.

Step 4: Raise your right knee to point to the sky and grip the big toe with your right hand as you go.

Step 5: Imitate an archer by drawing your right leg upwards and bringing your knee closer to your ear. Like an archer scrutinizing his target, your right arm should directly point to the toe, and your eyes should be fixed on the toe.

Step 6: While experiencing the stretch in your hamstrings, hold the pose for 15-30 seconds.

Step 7: Exhale slowly and return to your starting posture. Repeat the stance, this time stretching your left leg back. One cycle of

Archer position is now complete. Do it twice as part of a practice with other positions.

So, how will you know that your third eye is opening? There are some tell-tale signs.

- The Pressure in Your Head Is Increasing: You will begin to feel an increasing pressure between your brows, which is the most common indication of an open third eye. It could be a simple pulse or a strong sensation of something expanding in the center of your forehead. Spiritual experts urge you not to be concerned about this because it is absolutely harmless and will pass in time. They also claim that it may appear out of nowhere, and that a sensation of warmth on your forehead, as if someone is caressing you, is fairly common. So don't be alarmed if that happens.

- Increased foreknowledge of future events: You may have increased foresight of future occurrences. It could just be a slight feeling in your stomach that warns you that something bad is about to happen. Don't dismiss this gut feeling or intuition; instead, let it lead you ahead. It may be frightening at first, but once you realize that you have complete control over this ability, you will find it simpler to let it guide you.

- Light Sensitivity is a term that refers to a person's ability. As your third eye increases, you'll notice that you're more sensitive to light. This is due to the fact that you are seeing the world in a whole new light. You'll be able to notice distinct tints of colors in a more vivid manner as well. Everything that has to do with vision and light will be amplified. You might find that using polarized sunglasses helps.

- Gradual Alterations: You will reap the benefits of your new worldview because you are more in tune with your spiritual self. You'll notice that you're more relaxed, forgiving, and loving. These modifications may have an impact on your diet, since you will avoid processed foods in order to maintain your third eye health. You may not be able to pinpoint why these positive changes have occurred, but trust that your intuition and spiritual capabilities are driving you toward healthier lifestyle choices. Keep a watch on these changes since they are a solid sign that your third eye power is increasing.

- The Manifestation of Powers is a term used to describe the expression of your inner psychic abilities, your ability to sense and perceive things before they happen. Psychic abilities manifesting in people with an active third eye are not uncommon, contrary to popular assumption. Two of the most well-known instances are telepathy and clairvoyance. You should not be concerned, no matter how unfamiliar this is to you. Accept and nurture your abilities.

- Seeing Things That Aren't Immediately Obvious: Although knowing and seeing more than everyone else can be a hardship, your third eye can help you recognize half-truths and flashy statements. A restaurant that offers an all-you-can-eat buffet may appeal to the average person, but for you, it will be similar to an encouragement to consume more food than you require. This clarity of thought will allow you to make the best choices possible.

- Increased Self-Awareness: This third symptom is one that many people overlook. Your sense of inner self will improve if your third eye is open. As a result, rather than thinking of yourself as a mere human with interests, loves, and dislikes, you will consider yourself to be a part of the universe's fabric. This enhanced sense of self will allow you to rely more on yourself than on others, allowing you to live the prosperous life you've always desired.

If you don't know how to deal with the indicators of an active third eye, meditation and soothing activities that allow you to connect with your spiritual self will be your best asset. Whatever path you pick, remember that all of these expressions are gifts to be embraced rather than hidden.

Conclusion

In Indian mythology, *Shiva* is one of the three Gods responsible for the creation, upkeep and destruction of the world. Spiritual guru *Sadhguru* describes the meaning of *Shiva's* third eye and how it opens up to bring clarity and vision. He also tells a narrative about how *Shiva* used his third eye to burn *Kama*. In India, there is a god named *Kamadeva* who is the god of love and lust. *Kama* is the Sanskrit word for lust. According to legend, *Kama* concealed himself behind a tree and shot *Shiva* in the heart with an arrow. *Shiva* became agitated. As a result, he opened his fiery third eye and burned *Kama* to ashes. This is the version of the story that most people are familiar with.

But think about it: Does your lust come from within you or from behind a tree? Of course, it comes from within you. It's not just about the opposing sex when it comes to lust. Whether it's for sexuality, power, or position, every want is lust. Lust is defined as a feeling of inadequacy, a yearning for something that makes you feel like, "*If I don't have it, I am not complete.*"

The narrative of *Shiva* and *Kama* takes on a yogic dimension as a result of this. *Shiva* was pursuing Yoga, which meant he was striving not only to be complete, but also to be infinite. *Shiva* saw *Kama*, his own lust, approaching and burned it when he opened his third eye. Ash slowly flowed out of his body, indicating that everything inside had finally died. By opening his third eye, he was able to experience a dimension within himself that is beyond the physical, and all of his bodily compulsions vanished.

The third eye is an eye that can see things that aren't physical. Because it stops and reflects light, you can see it if you look at your hand. Because air does not block light, you cannot see it. However, if there was a small amount of smoke in the air, you would be able to see it because only something which prevents light can be seen. Nothing that enables light to pass through can be seen. The nature of the two sensory eyes is as follows.

The physical can be grasped by the sensory eyes. The only way to perceive something that isn't physical in nature is to go inside yourself. When we talk about the "third eye," we're referring to the ability to see something that the two sensory eyes can't.

The sensory eyes are pointed outward. Your interiority — the nature of yourself and your existence – is seen through the third eye. It's not a new appendage or a crack in your brow. The third eye is the dimension of perception through which one can perceive something which is beyond the physical.

You will be blessed with greater rewards as you progress in opening your third eye. To begin, you will develop razor-sharp intuition and the ability to tap into your inner wisdom.

Meditation and opening your third eye not only help you experience higher levels of consciousness, better self-awareness, and deeper emotional mastery, but it also tunes you to an innate skill that we all share—intuition. Third eye meditation has been practiced for generations in traditional cultural groups around the world, which see intuition as man's most important sense.

You'll notice early on in your meditation practice how much inner intellect you already have at your disposal. And once you begin to notice this inner wisdom, you'll have all the motivation you need to keep opening and activating your third eye to its full potential.

Your third eye will be able to tell you exactly what you need to improve your health, attract healthier relationships, and materialize professional and financial success. Your third eye intuition understands exactly why you picked this existence at this time. How much better would your life be if you could call on your inner-infinite-wisdom whenever you wanted?

Your third eye will also allow you to align with the law of attraction and manifest the life you want. We attract what we most believe in, according to this law. After all, like attracts like, and this is especially true when it comes to our minds. The essential power of the third eye lies in its potential to alter the nature of our ideas at their source. What's the end result? Worry, anxiety, and negative thinking are decreased. And once this mental baggage is removed, what replaces it will be of the greatest order, totally in sync with the all-pervasive law of attraction.

Your mental, emotional, and physical states will improve as your third eye opens up more and more, allowing you to attract higher-level souls into your life, resulting in new and better interactions on all levels. You will begin creating prosperity as naturally as breathing as your "meditation-activated" third eye illuminates the route to higher consciousness. A more conscious, meaningful, and deliberate life will emerge as a result.

Finally, in opening our third eye we learn that love, peace, and joy cannot be found outside of ourselves. While we may be on the lookout for external sources to provide us with more joy, peace, and love, our intuition leads us away from these fleeting springs. It directs us to the limitless reservoir of love, pleasure, and peace that exists inside us at all times. And it serves to draw us away from the incessant yearning for more and the misery we experience when we don't have enough. Finally, it softly nudges us towards our own inexhaustible source of love, serenity, and joy.

References

All you need to know about third eye meditation. (2019, December 10). *Times of India.* https://timesofindia.indiatimes.com/life-style/health-fitness/home-remedies/all-you-need-to-know-about-third-eye-meditation/articleshow/72458177.cms

Blavatsky, H.P., 1888, *The Secret Doctrine*, 2 vols., London: The Theosophical Publishing Company.

Goel, M. (2014). *Yoga Poses: Archer's Pose (Akarna Dhanurasana).* Workout Trends. https://workouttrends.com/archer-pose

Lokhorst, Gert-Jan, "Descartes and the Pineal Gland", *The Stanford Encyclopedia of Philosophy* (Fall 2020 Edition), Edward N. Zalta (ed.), URL = https://plato.stanford.edu/archives/fall2020/entries/pineal-gland/

Luke, J. A. (1997). *The Effect of Fluoride on the Physiology of the Pineal Gland.* University of Surrey.

Murphy, A. (2020a). *How to Awaken Your Third Eye.* Gaia.

Murphy, A. (2020b). *The Pineal Gland and The Third Eye Chakra.* Gaia. https://www.gaia.com/article/pineal-third-eye-chakra

Nadi Shodhan Pranayama. (2021). Art of Living. https://www.artofliving.org/in-en/yoga/breathing-techniques/alternate-nostril-breathing-nadi-shodhan

Schumacher, J. (2011). *Take Aim: 5 Steps to Archer Pose*. Outside. https://www.yogajournal.com/practice/advanced/advanced-pose-how-to/take-aim/

Signs Your Third Eye Is Starting To See. (2020). Holy City Sinner. https://holycitysinner.com/2020/01/22/signs-your-third-eye-is-starting-to-see/

Stokes, V. (2021). *How to Open Your Third Eye Chakra for Spiritual Awakening*. Healthline. https://www.healthline.com/health/mind-body/how-to-open-your-third-eye

The Sixth Chakra: Center of Intuition. (2021). 3HO Foundation. https://www.3ho.org/kundalini-yoga/chakras/eight-major-chakras/sixth-chakra-center-intuition

The Story of Shiva's Third Eye and Its Hidden Symbolism. (2021). Sadhguru.Org. https://isha.sadhguru.org/mahashivratri/shiva/shivas-third-eye-its-hidden-symbolism/

Wilcox, J.-C., 1985, *The Transmission and Influence of Qusta ibn Luqa's "On the Difference between Spirit and the Soul"*, Ph.D. thesis, City University of New York.

Zoldan, R. J. (2020). *Your 7 Chakras, Explained—Plus How to Tell if They're Blocked*. Well+good. https://www.wellandgood.com/what-are-chakras/